COUNTRIES IN OUR W

USA

Lisa Klobuchar

W
FRANKLIN WATTS

This edition published in 2012 by
Franklin Watts
338 Euston Road
London NW1 3BH

Franklin Watts Australia
Level 17/207 Kent Street
Sydney NSW 2000

Produced for Franklin Watts by
White-Thomson Publishing Ltd
+44 (0) 843 208 7460
www.wtpub.co.uk

Series consultant: Rob Bowden
Editor: Sonya Newland
Designer: Clare Nicholas
Picture researcher: Amy Sparks

A CIP catalogue record for this book is available
from the British Library.

Dewey Classification: 973.9'32

ISBN 978 1 4451 0812 4

Printed in Malaysia

Franklin Watts is a division of Hachette Children's
Books, an Hachette UK company

www.hachette.co.uk

Picture Credits
Corbis: 7 (Andrew Gombert/epa), 13 (Bettmann), 14
(Ed Kashi), 15 (Ed Kashi), 16 (Jeff Zelevansky/Reuters),
17 (John Gress/Reuters), 20 (Reuters), 23 (Steven
Georges/Press-Telegram), 25 (Matthew Cavanaugh/
epa), 28 (Guy Reynolds/Dallas Morning News).
Dreamstime: 4-5 (Michele Perbellini), 8 (Aliaksandr
Nikitsin), 9 (Ben Renard-Wiart), 10 (Elimitchell),
18–19 (Dreamshot); **FEMA News Photo:** 26 (Andrea
Booher); **iStock:** 29 (Jani Bryson); **NASA:** 21;
Shutterstock: 1 (Albert de Bruijn), 11 (Andy Z), 12
(Matt McClain), 19 (Byron W. Moore), 22 (Gary718),
24 (Albert de Bruijn), 27 (Christopher Halloran);
US Department of Defense: 6 (Edwin L. Wriston).

Contents

Introducing the USA

Its wealth and military strength make the United States of America the most powerful country in the world. Despite criticism by other countries over economic problems and unpopular wars fought in Afghanistan and Iraq, the USA still has a major influence on international economics and politics.

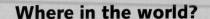

Where in the world?

Most of the USA lies in the middle part of the continent of North America. This is where 48 of the nation's 50 states are located. Two other states lie far away. Alaska is beyond the north-west border of Canada, the country to the north of the USA. Hawaii is made up of several islands in the South Pacific Ocean. Beyond the southernmost states lie Central and South America.

◀ *The Statue of Liberty is a symbol of the freedom that is one of the most treasured American values.*

IT'S A FACT!

The Statue of Liberty commemorates the signing of the Declaration of Independence in 1776, when America began a campaign against British rule. The 46-m (150-ft) statue (a gift from France) stands at the entrance to New York Harbor, welcoming ships to 'the land of the free'.

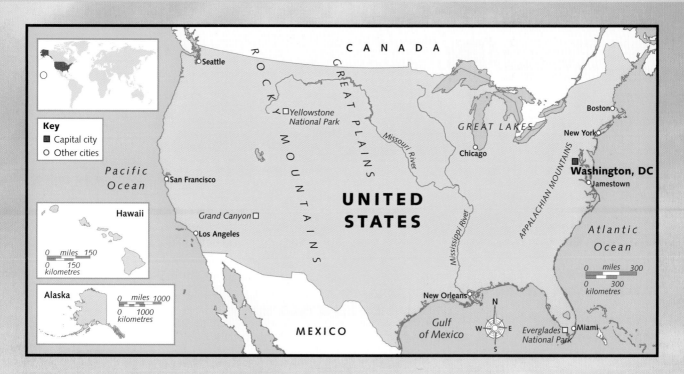

Key
■ Capital city
○ Other cities

A young nation

The USA was one of the first nations created when people moved away from their native countries and formed colonies overseas. About 400 years ago, people from Great Britain travelled across the ocean and first settled on the east coast of what is now the USA. In 1776, these settlers declared their independence from Britain, and after an eight-year war the USA officially became an independent country.

▲ *The USA, the world's third-largest country, shares borders with Canada in the north and Mexico in the south.*

A nation of immigrants

Throughout its history, the USA has attracted settlers from all over the world. People moved there to seek freedoms and opportunities they did not have in their own countries, and its many immigrant communities have all left their stamp on American life.

Global superpower

After the collapse of the USSR in the 1990s, the USA emerged as the only superpower in the world. But what makes it so powerful? For one thing, it is the richest country in the world. The value of US goods and services is significantly higher than that of China, the world's second largest economy.

BASIC DATA
Official name: **United States of America**
Capital: **Washington, D.C.**
Size: **9,826,630 sq km (3,794,083 sq miles)**
Population: **313,847,465**
Currency: **Dollar**

Military strength

The USA also has the mightiest military in the world. It spends over six times more on its armed forces than China, which ranks second in military expenditure. Despite this, China continues to grow in global power and influence, and will probably challenge the USA's status as the only superpower.

▼ *The US kept a strong military presence in Iraq until the end of 2011.*

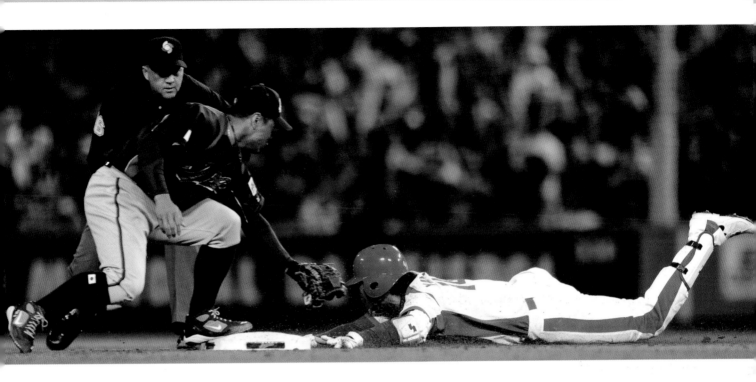

Troubled times

The USA started a war in Iraq in 2003, believing that the Iraqis were hiding powerful weapons known as 'weapons of mass destruction'. The war itself lasted only a few weeks, but it wasn't until 2011 that the last US troops were finally withdrawn. Although countries such as the UK supported the invasion of Iraq, others disagreed and many Americans protested against it, too. In 2008, poor investments caused some important financial companies in the USA to fail. Many other countries were affected as a result, and a worldwide recession began.

Cultural leader

One major way the USA makes its mark on the rest of the world is through its culture. American fast-food chains such as McDonalds and Pizza Hut thrive in many countries. American sports such as baseball and basketball have become popular throughout the world. People all over the globe enjoy and copy American music, art, fashion, film and television. However, not everyone appreciates the USA's influence on their countries' arts and culture, feeling that their own are lost as America's influence spreads.

▲ Japan and South Korea play in the final of the 2009 World Baseball Classic. American sports like this are enjoyed all over the world.

The USA covers the entire middle section of the continent of North America. It is the world's third largest country – only Russia and Canada are larger. The USA stretches from the Pacific Ocean in the west to the Atlantic Ocean in the east. It shares a long border with Canada in the north and with Mexico in the south.

East of the Mississippi

The Mississippi River forms a dividing line between the different landscapes of the USA. East of the Mississippi lie the temperate forests of the Midwest and Northeast regions. In the far eastern part of the country is a region of highlands with several forested mountain ranges. The land slopes down to the east coast, which has many sandy beaches.

▼ *With a surface area of 82,413 sq km (31,820 sq miles), Lake Superior is a major waterway for transport of goods, as well as a destination for tourists.*

THE HOME OF...

The Great Lakes

The Great Lakes – five large, freshwater lakes on the border with Canada in the north-central part of the USA – contain about 20 per cent of the world's fresh water. The largest of the Great Lakes, Lake Superior, is the largest freshwater lake in the world.

West of the Mississippi

A huge, flat region lies in the middle part of the country. Part of this region is called the Great Plains, a fairly dry grassland where few trees grow. The towering Rocky Mountains run from Alaska to Mexico. To the west of the Rockies is a region of deserts, dry lowlands and high plateaus. Mountain ranges and wide valleys make up the far western part of the country.

Climate

Most of the USA is in the Earth's temperate middle latitudes. This means that it has cool or cold winters and warm or hot summers. But the country has many different climates. Scorching deserts lie in the south-west. In the north-west are cool, green temperate rainforests. Alaska has an arctic climate, with bitterly cold winters and short, cool summers. Hawaii and Florida have a tropical climate, with warm temperatures all year round.

▼ *South-western USA is hot and dry. Here, in the desert of Utah, the wind has worn the sandstone into shapes such as pillars and arches.*

IT'S A FACT!

Hurricane Katrina struck the Gulf Coast of the USA in August 2005, destroying parts of the historic city of New Orleans in Louisiana, as well as damaging other coastal cities in Mississippi and Alabama. About 1,300 people died as a result of the storm, and it caused an estimated $125 billion in damage. In terms of economic damage, Katrina was the worst natural disaster in US history.

Protecting wildlife

The USA has hundreds of national parks and refuges, where the environment is conserved and wildlife protected. The largest refuge is the 81,000 sq km (31,250 sq mile) Yukon Delta National Wildlife Refuge in Alaska. In 2002 and 2003, President George W. Bush tried to pass laws that would allow oil companies to drill in the Alaskan Arctic National Wildlife Refuge. Many people were afraid of the damage this would do to the environment. The refuge is home to grizzly bears, caribou and polar bears, as well as many types of birds and fish. In the end the laws were not passed.

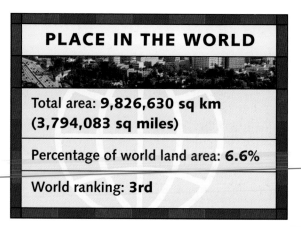

PLACE IN THE WORLD

Total area: 9,826,630 sq km (3,794,083 sq miles)
Percentage of world land area: 6.6%
World ranking: 3rd

▼ *Animals such as caribou (reindeer) and moose make their homes in freezing Alaska. The country's largest national parks lie in this relatively unpopulated area.*

▲ *In some big cities, such as Los Angeles, air pollution is so bad that a permanent smog hangs over them.*

Controlling pollution

The USA faces many environmental challenges. Pollution from factories, power plants, farms and cars endangers people's health and the natural environment. The USA sets pollution rules through the Environmental Protection Agency (EPA), but it is still the world's worst polluter and the biggest generator of waste. To tackle this problem, the US government has passed laws to control pollution, such as the Clean Air Act and the Clean Water Act.

IT STARTED HERE

Earth Day

Earth Day is a special day to make people aware of the environmental issues threatening our planet. It was first celebrated in the USA on 22 April 1970, after Senator Gaylord Nelson decided to organize a protest at how little was being done to protect the environment. Earth Day is now celebrated all over the world every year.

Population and migration

Many people call the USA a 'melting pot'. This means that people from all over the world have settled there and brought their unique traditions and beliefs, which have all influenced American culture today.

CAPTAIN
JOHN SMITH
GOVERNOR OF
VIRGINIA
1608

Colonial life

The first people to live in what is now the USA were Native Americans. They belonged to many different groups, each with its own traditions and beliefs. Beginning in the late 1500s, settlers from European countries began to arrive. From about 1600 to 1750, Europeans settled throughout the eastern part of the present-day USA. Most of them were from the UK, so the new land became a colony of Britain. The population also included large numbers of Dutch people, as well as those from France, Sweden, Germany and most other Western European countries. Some black Africans were brought against their will and put to work as slaves. Descendants of all these people make up the American population today.

Moving westwards

The United States of America was born after the colonists won a war of independence against Britain in 1783. The new country grew steadily over the next 100 years. In 1803, President Thomas Jefferson bought a huge piece of land in the middle of what is now the USA from France, which doubled the size of

◀ *This statue in Jamestown, Virginia, commemorates Captain John Smith, who helped establish the first permanent English settlement in America.*

the country. People began travelling west into lands that had previously been unexplored by Europeans. The US government gave away land on the prairies to people who would farm it. These people became known as homesteaders. The Native Americans, who had once moved freely across these lands, were driven on to controlled areas called reservations.

Waves of immigration

Throughout its history, the USA has welcomed millions of immigrants. From 1820 to 1870, about 7.5 million people arrived, many of them from Ireland and Germany. Then, from 1870 to 1916, about 25 million people moved to the USA, doubling its population. Most of them were from Eastern Europe and from China.

FAMOUS AMERICAN

Jane Addams
(1860–1935)

Jane Addams devoted her life to helping immigrants and the poor in the USA. She founded Hull House in Chicago in 1889. Here, immigrants learned the skills they needed to become citizens of the USA. Addams won the Nobel Peace Prize in 1931.

▼ *Immigrants arriving in America in the early twentieth century.*

The population today

In 1960, 83 per cent of Americans were white people who were born there. Most of the rest were black Americans descended from African slaves. By 2006, only 67 per cent of Americans were native-born whites. About 14 per cent were Hispanic (from the Spanish-speaking countries of Central America) and 12 per cent were black. About 12 per cent of the US population were immigrants. This most recent wave of immigration is still going on today.

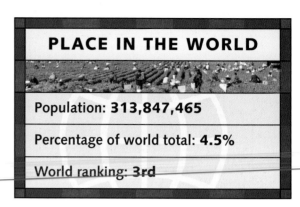

PLACE IN THE WORLD

Population: **313,847,465**

Percentage of world total: **4.5%**

World ranking: **3rd**

Where do Americans live?

The coastal regions along the Atlantic and Pacific oceans and the Gulf of Mexico are home to about 38 per cent of Americans. About 33 per cent live around the Great Lakes and in the Northeast region. Most of the rest live in the Rocky Mountain and Great Plains states. The area between Boston, Massachusetts and Washington, DC, is the most densely populated.

▼ *Hispanic immigrant workers pick beans in a field in Florida. People like these, from Latin America, make up the latest wave of immigrants to the USA.*

Americans on the move

Americans as a group move around more than people in the rest of the world. The average American moves 11 to 13 times in his or her life, mostly within the USA, but sometimes abroad. As different parts of the USA are made up of people from different ethnic backgrounds, such a mobile population helps Americans become familiar with different cultures, and creates the multicultural society that is typical of the USA.

▲ *The USA is one of the most multicultural countries in the world, with people from many ethnic backgrounds.*

Standard of living

Americans enjoy one of the highest standards of living in the world. But in some ways the USA does not meet the same standards as other developed countries. It has a higher divorce rate, lower educational performance, higher rates of crime and homelessness, and a higher infant mortality rate than many countries in Western Europe, for example.

GLOBAL LEADER

Immigration

The USA leads the world in immigration. In 2011, most newcomers came from Mexico, India, the Philippines, China and Colombia. Almost a third of the foreign–born people in the USA were from Mexico.

American fast food, pop music, television programmes, movies and clothing styles have spread across the globe. They all influence the culture and lifestyles of millions of people.

Freedom to be different

The people of the USA have a strong sense of shared culture. Most Americans speak English and have similar habits of dress, food and housing. At the same time, Americans descended from the different groups of early settlers are often proud of their individual heritage. The traditions of many countries, brought by millions of immigrants, have blended to create American culture. This makes Americans more tolerant than people in many other countries, and they have a strong belief in equality and freedom.

Personal space

Americans are unique among other Western cultures in their desire to live apart from others. Most Americans prefer to live in suburbs rather than in crowded cities.

▶ *As suburbs grew, shopping malls became popular as a way for people to get everything they needed under one roof.*

IT STARTED HERE

Shopping malls

The first modern, enclosed shopping mall was built in Edina, Minnesota, in 1956. It was the first mall to be built on more than one level and entirely enclosed. It became the model for nearly all shopping malls today.

The American dream

Since the mid 1900s, the typical 'American dream' has been to own a large house in the suburbs with at least one car. After the end of World War II in 1945, there was a large movement of people from the cities to the suburbs. This was largely because there was the space to 'spread out' – the USA is a large country and had not been settled for hundreds of years like many other countries.

A religious nation

People are free to follow any religion they want. Surveys show that about seven in 10 Americans believe in God, and around half of them say that religion is very important in their lives. Around 75% of Americans call themselves Christians, although not all of them are practising.

IT'S A FACT!

Christian churches in America have grown bigger over the last 20 years. A megachurch is a Christian church with more than 2,000 members. Services usually feature live music and videos projected on large screens. There are over 1,300 megachurches in the USA. About five million people attend services at megachurches across America each week.

▼ *This megachurch in Illinois can seat 7,000 people. Big screens allow everyone to see the preacher and to share in the experience.*

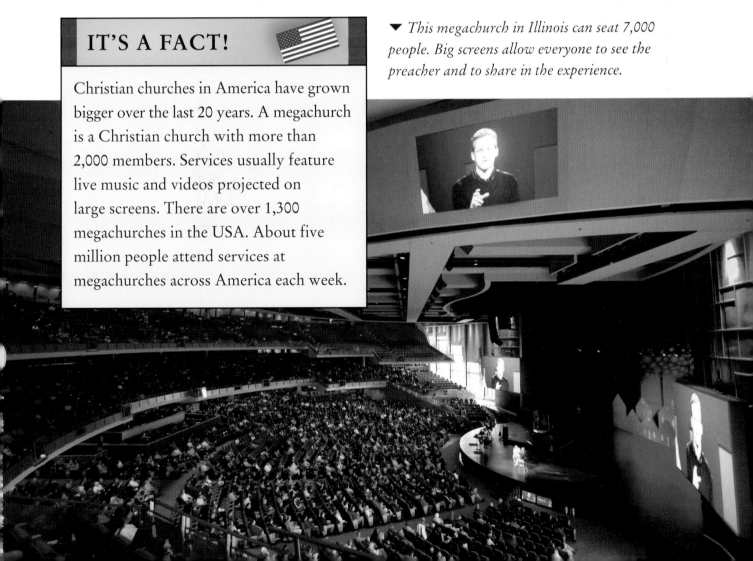

Festivals and celebrations

One of the most important national holidays in the USA is Independence Day, celebrated on 4 July every year to commemorate the adoption of the Declaration of Independence and freedom from British rule. Families and friends have picnics, and there are often fireworks displays. Thanksgiving is a harvest festival celebrated in November, to commemorate the Native Americans helping the early settlers by sharing their food with them.

GOING GLOBAL

Fast food, which started in America, has exploded around the world. McDonald's has over 33,000 restaurants worldwide in 118 countries. KFC, the fried chicken chain, is especially popular in China, where it operates over 3,000 stores.

A sporting nation

Americans are huge sports fans and sport is an important part of American culture. The most popular sports are American football, baseball, basketball and ice hockey, and the USA leads the world in these sports. Americans support their teams passionately, and championship games such as the Super Bowl (American football) and the World Series (baseball) attract thousands of fans to the live event and millions more who watch on television. Soccer – the most popular sport in the world – is not nearly as popular as other sports in the USA.

▼ *Crowds in the National Mall park in Washington, D.C. celebrate Independence Day on 4 July. Families gather for picnics and to watch fireworks after the sun sets.*

Film and music

American popular culture such as films, television and musical styles are its most famous exports. As the home of Hollywood, America has influenced the film industry in many other countries, but it is also known for creating high-quality television dramas

that are popular all over the world. Musical genres such as jazz, blues and country music were all born in the USA. Later, these were adapted and developed into modern styles such as rock 'n' roll, rap, soul and funk. Today, American film and pop stars are known all over the world, and are more famous than native stars in many countries.

THE HOME OF...

Hollywood

The area of Los Angeles, California, known as Hollywood is the heart of the world's film industry. The first film studio was set up here in 1909, and since then Hollywood has set the standard for blockbuster movies all over the world, making and releasing hundreds of films every year. Its influence is so widespread that the Indian film industry based in Mumbai has been nicknamed 'Bollywood'.

The USA has by far the largest economy in the world. The country is rich in resources, including fertile farmland, waterways, minerals and forests. The worldwide economic crisis in 2008 and 2009 caused the USA to slip into a recession. Since then the economy has slowly picked up but the government continues to face serious difficulties.

Free enterprise

The economy of the USA is based on free enterprise. This means that the people rather than the government manage the economy. The government makes some rules and laws, and controls some business activities to make sure that businesses operate fairly and that Americans get the goods and services they need for a safe, happy life. However, the people decide what to make, and how to make it; they decide what to sell, and for how much money.

▼ *Bill Gates – one of the richest men in the world – shows off Microsoft's Tablet PC.*

FAMOUS AMERICAN

Bill Gates
(b. 1955)

Bill Gates is a pioneer in the personal-computer industry. With a boyhood friend, Paul Allen, he founded Microsoft in 1975. They developed operating systems – programs that tell computers how to run. Today, Microsoft is the world's largest software company, selling the world's top operating system, Windows.

Growing service industries

As in other Western countries, the American service industry employs most of the workers and creates most of the country's wealth. Service industries are those that provide services for people rather than making products. In the early 2000s, 83 per cent of America's workers were employed in service industries, including property, tourism, healthcare, hotels, law firms, banking and restaurants.

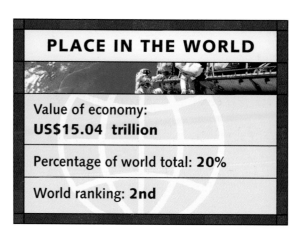

PLACE IN THE WORLD

Value of economy:
US$15.04 trillion

Percentage of world total: **20%**

World ranking: **2nd**

Hi-tech leader

The USA has long been known as a leader in technology, and this brings a lot of money into the economy. For the most part, it has led the world in advances in computers, medicine, spacecraft, air travel and military equipment. In particular, it led the way in space technology. America was the first country to put a man on the Moon, and it now plays an important part in the International Space Station (ISS), a joint project between the USA, Russia, Japan, Canada and countries of the European Space Agency.

▼ *An American astronaut and one from the European Space Agency work on the ISS, an international space project.*

Global economy

The USA is the world's biggest importer and its second biggest exporter of goods and services. Recently, the US economy has become more tied up with that of other countries. For example, US companies import parts such as car parts from other countries. The vehicles are put together in the USA and the finished products are shipped abroad to be sold. The USA's top trading partners in 2010 were Canada, Mexico, China and Japan.

▲ *The Port of Miami is one of the largest in the USA. Both container ships for importing and exporting goods, and cruise ships use this port.*

Manufacturing

Businesses that produce goods such as steel, cars, computers, toys and clothing are called manufacturers. The USA is a world leader in manufacturing, and American products – from Apple iPods and Disney merchandise to clothing – can be found everywhere. However, there are now fewer workers in the manufacturing industry than ever before. Over the past 30 years, many American companies have built factories in other countries, such as China, Mexico and India, where labour costs are lower. This means that many American manufacturing jobs have been lost.

GOING GLOBAL

American children play with mostly foreign-made toys. Almost 90 per cent of all toys sold in the USA are imported, and China supplies almost 90 per cent of those imports.

The tourist industry

Tourism is big business in the USA. In fact, America earns more from tourists than any other country in the world. In 2011, tourism brought nearly US$153 billion into the US economy. Because the USA is such a large country, it has many different attractions for tourists. Some come to enjoy the sunshine and beaches in places like California, or to go to world-famous amusement parks like Disneyland. Others visit the many national parks and natural sites like the Grand Canyon. Still others visit big cities like New York to go to the museums and galleries – or just to enjoy the shopping.

Economic hard times

In 2007, the US economy seemed strong, but there were signs of trouble. Prices for items like petrol and services such as healthcare were rising, but people's wages were not rising. By late 2008, many businesses, including major banks and car companies, had failed. People started to compare this economic crisis to the Great Depression – a period of severe economic hardship that lasted from the late 1920s to the late 1930s. In 2008 and early 2009, the US government spent more than US$1.2 trillion to rescue companies and create jobs, resulting in a slow economic recovery.

▼ *Disneyland, California, is one of the world's top tourist attractions, with around 15 million visitors per year.*

Government and politics

The USA was formed a little more than 230 years ago, but its constitution – the document that describes the basic principles of how the country will be run – is the oldest written constitution still in use. It has lasted such a long time because it has ensured a stable government and a good life for most Americans.

Power from the people

According to the constitution, the power is held by the people of America. It states clearly what powers the government has, which include the authority to collect taxes, to maintain the armed forces and to carry on trade with other countries. The constitution also limits the power of the government by granting American citizens certain rights. For example, the government cannot tell people what religion they must follow or punish people for what they say or write publicly.

THE HOME OF...

The White House

The White House is the home and official workplace of the US president. It is situated in Washington, DC, and was built between 1792 and 1800. Not far from the White House is the United States Capitol, which is where Congress – the Senate and the House of Representatives – meets.

▼ *The White House has become a global symbol of democracy.*

Federal system

The USA has a federal system of government. This means that the country is made up of separate states united under the federal, or national, government. Each state can make its own laws on matters such as education or punishments for crimes, but state laws cannot conflict with laws passed by the federal government – and all laws must follow the rules of the constitution.

▲ *The United States Congress is jointly made up of the House of Representatives and the Senate. The men and women of Congress are elected by the people in their home state.*

Three branches of government

The US government is made up of three branches: executive, legislative and judicial. The president of the USA is the leader of the executive branch, which carries out the laws. Two groups of lawmakers – the House of Representatives and the Senate – make up the legislative branch. They write and pass new laws. The judicial branch is made up of courts led by judges. The judicial branch settles disagreements about laws. It also decides whether laws passed by the House and Senate follow the rules of the US constitution. Each branch of the government can undo actions by the other branches, which makes sure that no one branch can grow too powerful.

World superpower

The USA's position as the world's only superpower means that it has a lot of influence over international affairs. Other countries will often follow the USA's lead in matters of war, international politics and economic policy, and decisions made in the USA can have a far-reaching effect. The power the USA has makes it a model for other nations, but it also sometimes makes it a target for criticism.

Terrorist attacks

On 11 September 2001, Islamic terrorists destroyed the World Trade Center, two large office towers in New York City. In response to this, the US government declared a 'War on Terror', determined to catch the people who had carried out the attacks and prevent such an event happening again.

GOING GLOBAL

The US government suspected that Iraq was involved in the terrorist attacks and claimed that the country had weapons of mass destruction. The USA invaded Iraq in 2003 and overthrew its leader, Saddam Hussein. Several other countries were drawn into the war. The UK, Australia, Poland and Denmark also sent troops to Iraq, but countries such as France, Germany and Russia were against the invasion.

▲ *Firefighters search through the rubble after the 9/11 terrorist attacks in New York.*

The War on Terror

To prevent another terrorist attack on US soil, the government took drastic measures. It passed laws making it legal to spy on Americans. It started wars in Iraq and Afghanistan, where Islamic terrorists were believed to be. It also imprisoned many suspected terrorists in a prison camp at Guantanamo Bay in Cuba.

Promising change

When Barack Obama became president in January 2009, he promised to change many policies that Americans were unhappy with. In particular he announced that he would bring all troops home from Iraq, which was completed at the end of 2011. He is also working with others to withdraw US troops from Afghanistan. He has visited the Middle East and continues in his efforts to improve relations with the Islamic world. He has battled to improve healthcare provision for all US citizens, regardless of income.

FAMOUS AMERICAN

Barack Obama (b. 1961)

Barack Obama grew up in Hawaii and Indonesia, the son of an American mother and a Kenyan father. He entered politics in 1996 when he was elected to the Illinois Senate, and in 2005 he became a US senator. In January 2009, he became the US president – the first African-American to hold that position.

▶ *Many Americans felt that President Barack Obama's election was a turning point for the country, and that the political and economic situation would begin to improve.*

It is likely that the USA will continue to be the world's most powerful nation for some years, despite the rise of China as a global power. Over the next few years, Americans' living standards may improve, but those in other countries may become more equal to the USA. The US population will also change, as immigration rises and the birth rate slows.

Changing face of the nation

In 2005, about 12 per cent of the US population was foreign-born. By 2050, that number is expected to rise to 19 per cent. It is estimated that 67 million people will immigrate to the USA in the next 40 years. By 2020, it is thought that the number of children of foreign-born Hispanics will have doubled from what it was in 2000. These people may not have equal education and job opportunities with other groups, so the gap between rich and poor may grow wider.

▼ *Immigrant children hold up the certificates that prove they are now American citizens.*

Population growth

Unlike many developed countries in Europe and Asia, where populations are declining, the population of the USA is still growing. People are also living longer than ever before, and in coming years, the number of senior citizens will grow. By 2020 the US Census Bureau expects that about one in every five people will be 65 or older. There will be fewer younger workers to create wealth for the country, so the USA will be challenged to find ways to care for its ageing population. More older Americans will also be working well beyond today's retirement age of 65.

The future of trade

Most experts believe that all over the world, trade among different countries will go up. The USA will continue to be a part of that growth. In 2011, imports made up about 14 per cent of the total US economy. Exports of American-made products were about 13 per cent. The US government believes that by 2027, this will have grown dramatically, and imports will be about 26 per cent of the US economy and exports will be about 27 per cent.

▲ *Schoolchildren say the Pledge of Allegiance before the US flag. Young people (under the age of 20) currently make up a quarter of the US population, but that balance is expected to shift in the near future.*

Glossary

Christianity a religion that follows the teachings of Jesus Christ.

colony a territory under the immediate political control of a nation.

conservation protecting and preserving the natural environment and wildlife.

constitution a document that lays out the main laws of a nation. Laws are not allowed to be passed that contradict a country's constitution.

continent one of the Earth's seven great land masses – Africa, Antarctica, Asia, Australia, Europe, North America and South America.

democracy a form of government in which people vote for the leaders they wish to represent them.

economy the financial system of a country or region, including how much money is made from the production and sale of goods and services.

ethnic group a group of people who identify with each other and feel they share a history.

export to transport products or materials abroad for sale or trade.

immigrant a person who has moved to another country to live.

import to bring in goods or materials from a foreign country for sale.

infant mortality the number of children who die before reaching adulthood in a particular country.

minerals natural rocks that come from the ground.

plateau a relatively flat, high expanse of land.

pollution spoiling the environment with man-made waste, such as gases from vehicle emissions or chemicals from factories or pesticides.

prairie a large expanse of grassland, where few trees grow.

rainforest a forest that receives more than 1 m (3.3 ft) of rainfall spread evenly throughout the year.

recession an extended period when the economy of a country slows down.

reservations special areas of land set aside for the Native American people after they were driven off their native land by white settlers.

resources things that are available to use, often to help develop a country's industry and economy. Resources could be minerals, workers (labour), water, or many other things.

suburbs areas on the outskirts of cities that are less built-up than city centres.

terrorist a person who uses violence or causes fear, to try and change a political system or policy.

USSR Union of Soviet Socialist Republics. A communist country in eastern Europe and northern Asia. In 1991, the USSR split into independent countries, including Russia.

Further information

Books

Attack on America (Dates with History)
by Brian Williams
(Cherrytree Books, 2007)

Celebrate USA
by Robyn Hardyman
(Franklin Watts, 2009)

The USA (Looking at Countries)
by Kathleen Pohl
(Franklin Watts, 2009)

USA (Letters from Around the World)
by Cath Senker
(Cherrytree Books, 2007)

Websites

http://www.americaslibrary.gov/
The Library of Congress site with information for kids about American people, states and historical events.

http://www.travelforkids.com/Funtodo/United_States/usa.htm
Take a journey through the USA with this fun site, travelling from Alaska to Hawaii.

http://www.socialstudiesforkids.com/subjects/economics.htm
Get to grips with economics with this site, where topics such as money, trade and budgets are explained.

Every effort has been made by the publisher to ensure that these websites contain no inappropriate or offensive material. However, because of the nature of the Internet, it is impossible to guarantee that the content of these sites will not be altered. We strongly advise that Internet access is supervised by a responsible adult.

Index

Numbers in **bold** indicate pictures